Ten Po
about Angels

ex libris

Candlestick Press

Published by:

Candlestick Press,
Diversity House, 72 Nottingham Road, Arnold, Nottingham NG5 6LF
www.candlestickpress.co.uk

Design and typesetting by Craig Twigg

Printed by Ratcliff & Roper Print Group, Nottinghamshire, UK

Selection and Introduction © Romalyn Ante, 2022

Cover illustration © Sarah Kirby, 2022
www.sarahkirby.co.uk

Candlestick Press monogram © Barbara Shaw, 2008

© Candlestick Press, 2022

Donation to Starlight Children's Foundation
www.starlight.org.uk

ISBN 978 1 913627 13 3

Acknowledgements

The poems in this pamphlet are reprinted from the following books, all by
permission of the publishers listed unless stated otherwise. Every effort has been
made to trace the copyright holders of the poems published in this book. The
editor and publisher apologise if any material has been included without
permission or without the appropriate acknowledgement, and would be glad to be
told of anyone who has not been consulted.

Thanks are due to all the copyright holders cited below for their kind permission:

Ellen Bass, *Indigo* (Copper Canyon Press, 2020) copyright © 2020 by Ellen Bass.
Reprinted with the permission of The Permissions Company, LLC on behalf of
Copper Canyon Press www.coppercanyonpress.org. Philip Gross, *The Thirteenth
Angel* (Bloodaxe Books, 2022) www.bloodaxebooks.com. Susan Harris, poem
first published here, by kind permission of Ian Parks. Ian Parks, *The Exile's
House* (Waterloo Press, 2013) by kind permission of the author. Cheryl Pearson,
Oysterlight (Pindrop Press, 2017). Pascale Petit, *Tiger Girl* (Bloodaxe Books,
2020) www.bloodaxebooks.com. Roger Robinson, *A Portable Paradise* (Peepal
Tree Press, 2019). Joanna Sedgwick, first published in this pamphlet, by kind
permission of the author.

Thanks are also due to Ian Parks, who came up with the idea for this pamphlet
and suggested some of the poems that have been included.

All permissions cleared courtesy of Suzanne Fairless-Aitken
c/o Swift Permissions swiftpermissions@gmail.com

Where poets are no longer living, their dates are given.

Introduction

For centuries, poets have explored the idea of faith and religion, the divine and the spiritual, and angels have been one of their most beloved subjects.

Ten Poems about Angels contains beautiful, lyrical, and engaging works that focus on both celestial angels and angelic qualities, from Emily Dickinson's divine 'Angels, in the Morning' to Roger Robinson's earthly angels in his poem 'On Nurses'.

I have chosen these unforgettable poems for their imaginative energy and emotional impact; they take us to many places and introduce us to different, engrossing characters. In Cheryl Pearson's 'Interview With An Angel, After The Fall,' the celestial being wishes to experience a very human emotion, the "exhilarating terror" of falling in love in which "everything came glass-clear" and "suddenly dangerous". In Pascale Petit's 'Her Half Indian Back', the speaker's profound love for her grandmother flashes back when she drives through rural India and witnesses the women balancing "firewood on their heads", reminding her of how her grandmother carried her "over the channel as she walked through the water / to take me to safety".

I adore each of the poems in this selection and the range of subjects they explore: there are poems about a holiday angel, tiny angels, and angelic qualities of humans and animals. There are poems that will give you significant insight and poems that will leave you with a sense of wonder. The collection is a testament that something beautiful and magnanimous can emerge from seemingly banal and mundane things. As Philip Gross describes in 'The Angel of the Slight', "the melt / of one snowflake… begins the avalanche — ".

Romalyn Ante

Everyday Angels

On Nurses

Surely this is more a calling than a job. The doldrums of the nightshift pierced with the odd life-threatening injury, applying pressure to a gaping wound. Their nurses' shoes clip-clopping down the halls, the thoughts of patients suffering or dead following them back home. Surely they know that life is random, how death can creep up on the innocent. But how their instincts can sometimes pull spirits back from the brink into their bodies. Like midwives to the spirit. In that moment, do they forget the training and think, if I do this, perhaps they will live? Can you train instinct? I'm not sure. They see it all: the birth, the death, the vomit, the blood, the shock, the diseased, the perturbed, the pain, the smiles. I see them pressing their uniforms for the next shift, washing their hands with a soap that makes their palms peel.

Roger Robinson

Her Half Indian Back

Sit up straight was her mantra,
my Gran of the correct posture
who wore her father's medals, chest out,
as she carried the Legion banner.

Only when I drove through rural India
did I see the women, all rod-backed,
balancing firewood on their heads,
a hay-bale, four bags of cement –

only then did I see her carrying me, not
in her womb, but on her head, held high
over the Channel as she walked
through water to take me to safety.

Pascale Petit

Kiss

When Lynne saw the lizard floating
in her mother-in-law's swimming pool,
she jumped in. And when it wasn't
breathing, its body limp as a baby
drunk on milk, she laid it on her palm
and pressed one fingertip to its silky breast
with just about the force you need
to test the ripeness of a peach, only quicker,
a brisk little push with a bit of spring in it.
Then she knelt, dripping wet in her Doc Martens
and camo T-shirt with the neck ripped out,
and bent her face to the lizard's face,
her big plush lips to the small stiff jaw
that she'd pried apart with her opposable thumb,
and she blew a tiny puff into the lizard's lungs.
The sun glared against the turquoise water.
What did it matter if she saved one lizard?
One lizard more or less in the world?
But she bestowed the kiss of life,
again and again, until
the lizard's wrinkled lids peeled back,
its muscles roused its own first breath
and she set it on the hot cement
where it rested a moment
before darting off.

Ellen Bass

To my Angel of Persistence

It is not my whooping cough
nor the lizard on fire pattering inside my lungs

that hauls me out of bed this morning,
but your tail that wags, pelting the wall,

my bedside table. Your deep stare—a sign
that despite this body tired of being tired,

and the clock that has been twined back,
I must still get up, put the pink leash

around your neck, and step into the light
of another morning in this landlocked town,

where a devotion of swans circles above.
We turn right to find the old man

who wears a Beatles cap is still sweeping
his neighbour's yard, but never mending

his own wooden fence that buckled
during the last windstorm.

The Victorian house before the cul-de-sac
has now got a modern door. But the lady

who wheels the bin out still wears
fake eyelashes thick as peacock fluff.

And isn't this what we live for?
To seek not for miracles, but for signs

that this life is still worth an expedition?
We walk on this pavement, graced

with last night's rain and assurance
that our story, no matter how painful,

is the right one for us.
Thank you, my angel of persistence,

for always pulling the lead
despite the gout in your back paw,

for living as if you're still in your prime—
dark brown gaze so alive,

chasing after something that sprints
along the brick wall, then disappears.

Romalyn Ante

The Angel of the North

I loved the concept
from the start: a high place
banking on the motorway
with something huge
and rusting rising there
as if the north
had gathered to itself
a new identity.
So when the sunlight lifted
and the traffic slowed

I looked up half-expectant
to make out – not quite a statue
but a landmark certainly,
casting a shadow over
love and death, the surge of cars,
and all the final things.
I glimpsed our destination
in the rear-view glass
and in my heartbeat heard
the pulse of outspread wings.

Ian Parks

Celestial Angels

'Angels, in the early morning'

Angels, in the early morning
May be seen the Dews among,
Stooping — plucking — smiling — flying
Do the Buds to them belong?

Angels, when the sun is hottest
May be seen the sands among,
Stooping — plucking — sighing — flying
Parched the flowers they bear along.

Emily Dickinson (1830 – 1886)

The Angel of the Slight

and Almost – of the least rank, below
the Dominions, the Powers, the Thrones:

the Nuances, the angels of fine tuning,
of each, any, moment in its balancing

along the Bridge of One Hair; one petal,
oyster-pink, tipped from the climbing rose

to fall, under mere weight of sunlight; the melt
of one snowflake that begins the avalanche –

the most quietly militant of angels, in their minute
near-imperceptible rebuttal of the brag and bray

of big simplicity, its marching orders. Angel of the caught
breath, of the comma or the careful line break or

small word, barely bearing a meaning, that marks,
that makes, a change in the momentum of the world.

Philip Gross

Interview With An Angel, After The Fall

What was it like?
I imagine like falling in love – an exhilarating terror,

in which everything came glass-clear,
in which everything was suddenly dangerous.

I am a creature constructed entirely of love,
but I have no heart. Even still, I'd swear

I felt it beat the whole way down
with bone-breaking rhythm.

How did I feel when my wings fell away?
Like a fish pulled bloodily from its element.

I hung between stars, once, rowed the light home.
Then I fell, and the sky let me go,

the breath of God
still hot on the back of my neck.

How does it feel to be human, at last?
Like thunder being born.

Like a new lamb trying, and failing,
to find its legs.

Cheryl Pearson

Guardians

Every now and then, one will follow you.
A body of light in the corner of your eye,
a strand of feather brushing your neck.

Sometimes you'll feel a thickening of the air,
a presence beside you, as you peel an orange
or button a shirt, other times, nothing.

They will wait with you,
for a lover to arrive or the kettle to boil,
biding their time, wrapped in whiteness.

And in that terrible moment,
the one where you hold your breath,
one of them will step in and breathe for you.

Joanna Sedgwick